Playing Sk...

Story by Dawn McMillan
Illustrations by Pat Reynolds

One day Ella said,
"Can we go ten-pin bowling today, please Mum?"

"Yes," said Mum. "Bowling is fun!"

"Grandma, you like bowling, too," said Ella.

3

Mum and Grandma and Ella got into the car.

Rrrr…**rrrr**…rrr… went the car!

"Oh, no!" said Mum.
"The car will not go!
We can't go bowling today."

5

They all went inside the house.

"Grandma!" said Ella.
"We can play ten-pin bowling here at **home**.
I will get my skittles."

7

"The skittles can go here like this," said Grandma.

Ella ran back to the chair.

"Look out!" she said.
"Here comes the ball."

9

"Clever girl, Ella," said Mum.

"You made four skittles go down."

"It's your go, Mum," said Ella.

11

Mum made **one** skittle go down!

"I'm not very good, am I?" she said.

13

Grandma looked at the skittles.

"Here comes the ball," she said.

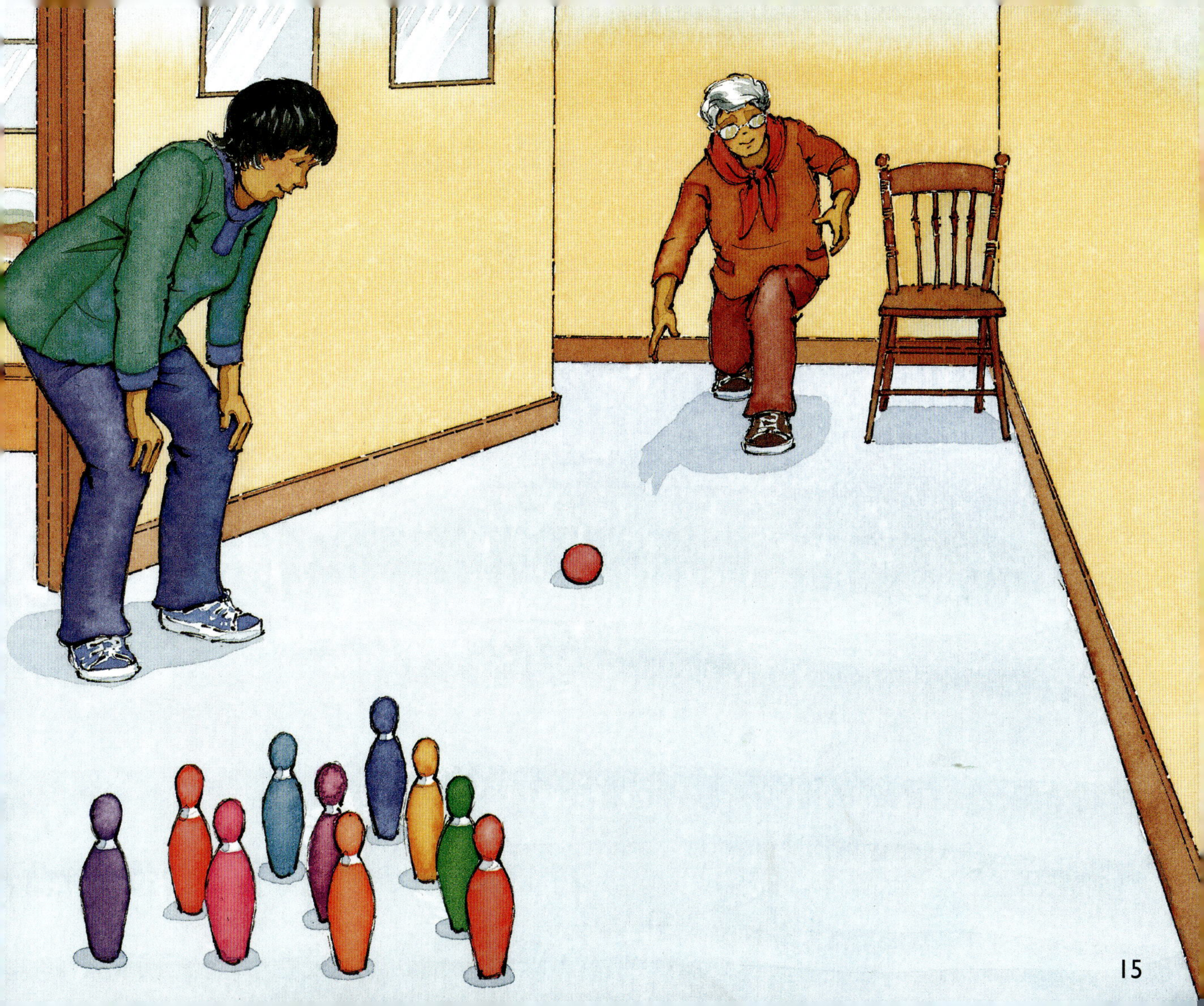

"Grandma, you hit **all** the skittles!" said Ella.

"Bowling at home is fun."